Chapter 1

TERRORISTS ATTACK THE UNITED STATES

As the day began, September 11, 2001, seemed like any other in the United States. Passengers boarded flights. People went to work, kids went to school, and businesses prepared to open. However, a series of terrorist attacks in New York City; Washington, DC; and Pennsylvania soon shocked the United States and the world.

That morning, 19 al-Qaeda terrorists boarded four commercial airplanes as passengers. The terrorists then hijacked the planes mid-flight. They crashed two of the planes into the Twin Towers of the World Trade Center (WTC) complex in New York City. A third plane hit the Pentagon in Washington, DC. The fourth crashed in a field near Shanksville, Pennsylvania, after passengers fought back against the hijackers.

These events are known as the 9/11 terrorist attacks. They killed nearly 3,000 people. This

AL-QAEDA

Al-Qaeda is an Islamist terrorist group. Its members believe that Middle Eastern countries should enforce strict laws based on Islam. Al-Qaeda believes in using violence to achieve this goal. People who follow Islam are called Muslims. Many Muslims do not agree with al-Qaeda's views. In fact, most Muslims think al-Qaeda's beliefs and actions go against the teachings of Islam.

included everyone aboard each plane and hundreds of people who were in the buildings when they were hit. It also included dozens of first responders who entered the buildings to fight the fires and help people evacuate.

Ground Zero

Shortly after the planes hit the WTC, both of the Twin Towers collapsed. In the aftermath, the WTC complex became known as Ground Zero. The twisted, burning wreckage made downtown New York City look like a war zone. For days, workers and volunteers searched the debris for survivors. Then, crews began the long, difficult task of clearing the wreckage.

Ground Zero looks much different today than it once did. Streets bustle with people. New buildings rise where the destroyed buildings once stood. However, a 9/11 memorial and museum ensure that the day's attacks will never be forgotten. Ground

Zero has become a solemn space to honor victims and heroes. But before the attacks, the area was a bustling hub of business.

The World Trade Center

On the morning of September 11, thousands of people were arriving to work at the WTC complex in New York City. It was located in the busiest and most densely populated part of the city. The seven buildings that made up the complex held major law firms and finance companies, among many other businesses. The Twin Towers were known as 1 WTC and 2 WTC.

Bystanders in New York City watched in horror as the Twin Towers burned and collapsed.

The North Tower

At 8:46 a.m., workers on the upper floors of 1 WTC, also called the North Tower, felt the building shake. The hijacked American Airlines Flight 11 had flown into the building, leaving a gaping hole at floors 93 through 99. Everyone aboard the plane and hundreds more in the building were killed instantly.

Emergency dispatchers took hundreds of emergency calls made from inside and around the North Tower. They sent firefighters, police officers, and paramedics to begin evacuating the building. These first responders were trained to respond to fires in high-rise buildings. Some had likely even responded to a different attack on the WTC eight years earlier.

That attack occurred on February 26, 1993. Terrorists parked a truck with a bomb inside it in a parking garage under the WTC. The blast created a large hole beneath the complex. Six people were killed and 1,000 were injured. Unfortunately, the number of injuries and deaths during the 2001 attacks would far surpass these numbers.

The South Tower

As North Tower evacuations continued, officials declared that 2 WTC, also called the South Tower, was secure. South Tower workers who had started evacuating due to the crash in the North Tower returned to their offices. At this point, it was assumed that the North Tower crash had been an accident.

Both planes that crashed into the Twin Towers were Boeing 767 airplanes.

But at 9:03 a.m., the hijacked United Airlines Flight 175 flew into the

South Tower. It hit floors 77 through 85. This second crash made it clear that the United States was facing an attack like none it had ever known before. With their building now on fire, South Tower workers began evacuating again. Despite their fear, they moved in orderly lines down the stairwells.

Huge explosions in the Twin Towers sent glass, metal, and other debris raining down.

People leaving the North Tower evacuated in a similar calm, orderly fashion. Many people escaping from upper floors of both buildings were badly burned. As they hurried down the stairs, firefighters ran up to look for more survivors.

Outside the buildings, survivors were met with confusion. Debris fell from both buildings onto the ground below, seriously injuring and killing many people. Police officers and paramedics instructed people with minor injuries to walk to nearby hospitals. Those with more serious injuries were quickly loaded into ambulances.

The South Tower begins to collapse.

Chapter 2

THE TOWERS FALL

News of the attacks spread locally within minutes. Blocks from the WTC, hundreds gathered in the streets to see the damage. They stared up in awe, some weeping, as the towers burned. Then, at 9:59 a.m., the top of the South Tower leaned to one side. Suddenly, there was a loud boom. In just ten seconds, the entire building collapsed.

Dust and Debris

Police on the streets shouted for people to run as the collapse created a massive cloud of smoke, dust, and debris. The sunny day turned dark as the cloud blocked the sky. Thick dust filled the air and covered people head to toe. Shoes littered the streets, abandoned by people as they ran.

At the scene, first responders were buried beneath piles of debris. They struggled to breathe in the hot dust. Large chunks of the building's steel and concrete frame had also come crashing down onto the street, crushing people and damaging nearby buildings. This included 7 WTC, which collapsed later that evening following multiple fires in the surrounding debris.

The End of the Twin Towers

People in the North Tower heard a loud roar and felt their building shake as the South Tower collapsed. Evacuations continued, with

People covered in dust from the collapse helped each other get to safety.

survivors spilling out into an unrecognizable wasteland. Firefighters in the North Tower were also told by their fire chiefs to evacuate. However, many did not hear the orders or did not have time to escape. Less than half an hour after the South Tower collapsed, the ground around the North Tower began to rumble. At 10:28 a.m., the North Tower also collapsed. The Twin Towers were gone.

2001 VS. TODAY

In 2001, firefighters were unable to fight the fires at Ground Zero after the towers collapsed. This is because the collapse destroyed water mains in the area. This reduced the water pressure, so firefighters didn't have enough water to fight the fires. Today, all Fire Department of the City of New York (FDNY) fire trucks have pumps that can take water from the nearby rivers to use in fighting fires.

Evacuating Lower Manhattan

First responders once again found themselves coated with choking dust. Many of them and other survivors wandered the scene in a daze. At 11:02 a.m., New York City mayor Rudolph "Rudy" Giuliani urged the public to evacuate the downtown area, known as Lower Manhattan. People left on foot and by water, the WTC smoking behind them. First responders and reporters coined a new name for the WTC site: Ground Zero.

Hundreds of people walked across the Brooklyn Bridge to get out of Manhattan. The bridge connects the boroughs of Manhattan and Brooklyn.

The Search for Survivors

In the hours after the attacks, the search for survivors at Ground Zero officially began. Many hoped that air pockets within the rubble could have protected people from being crushed. Because the wreckage was at risk of further collapse, workers sorted through the debris by hand rather than bringing in heavy excavating equipment. This careful digging reduced the risk of the large debris collapsing on top of survivors. By September 12, twenty survivors had been recovered from Ground Zero. These included eleven firefighters and two police officers.

Every day there were rumors that more survivors had been recovered or could be heard beneath the rubble. However, these rumors were proved false. "The recovery effort continues, and the hope is still there that we might be able to save some lives," Mayor

Giuliani told reporters on September 16. "But the reality is that in the last several days we haven't found anyone." Although workers didn't know it at the time, the last survivor had been found on September 12. Office worker Genelle Guzman-McMillan was pulled from the wreckage 27 hours after the buildings fell.

Political Leaders Visit Ground Zero

In the days after September 11, local, national, and international political leaders toured Ground Zero. These included French President Jacques Chirac, New York Senators Hillary Clinton and Chuck Schumer, and mayor of Jerusalem Ehud Olmert. Mayor Giuliani and New York governor George E. Pataki led these leaders through the site.

Specially trained dogs helped rescuers search the rubble for survivors.

On September 14, President George W. Bush toured Ground Zero. He first viewed the wreckage by helicopter with Giuliani and Pataki. Then, the men toured the site on foot. Bush was not scheduled to make a speech that day. However, during the tour, he grabbed a megaphone and climbed onto a burned fire truck.

President Bush (*center*) speaking to those working at Ground Zero

As Bush thanked the workers, someone in the crowd shouted that he couldn't hear the president. Bush responded, "I can hear you! The rest of the world hears you! And the people who knocked these buildings down will hear all of us soon." Bush's unplanned speech energized workers and people across the country as the cleanup at Ground Zero continued.

Wreckage of the World Trade Center

Chapter 3

CLEANUP

In the aftermath of the attacks, the wreckage of the WTC complex was referred to as "the Pile." The Pile was 16 acres (6.5 ha) of jagged steel beams, chunks of concrete, broken glass, and other rubble. It was several stories high in some places.

The Pile was also unstable. Falling debris had punched a large hole through the WTC plaza. So, the wreckage was piled in this hole instead of on solid ground. Fires deep within the hole burned for more than three months after the attacks.

Cleanup crews faced great danger at Ground Zero. Work was so dangerous that some workers wrote their names and phone numbers on their arms. This way, they could be easily identified if they fell into the hole or were crushed.

A Long Process

Cleanup continued over the next months. Those working at the site included firefighters, police

At first, workers carefully dug into the wreckage with shovels and used buckets to remove debris.

officers, and ironworkers. Ground Zero was divided into four sections, with fire department officials assigning workers to each section. Work also included cleaning and decontaminating nearby buildings that had been filled with dust. Volunteers staffed kitchens to feed workers and hand out water.

As the Pile stabilized, workers were able to bring in heavy equipment, including cranes and excavators, to help remove the wreckage. Ironworkers cut down steel beams. The WTC complex's four remaining buildings, which had been damaged beyond repair, were torn down. When bodies of victims were found, workers stopped and removed their helmets to honor the dead. Then the remains were carefully removed from the rubble.

Artifacts and Remains

Nearly 1.8 million tons (1.6 million t) of debris was loaded onto trucks and taken by barge to the Fresh Kills Landfill in Staten Island, New York. There, landfill workers sorted through the wreckage. They separated out personal belongings and other artifacts. Some days they combed through 7,000 tons (6,350 t) of debris.

The landfill workers sent recovered artifacts to be stored in an empty hangar at John F. Kennedy International Airport in Queens. Artifacts included tattered clothes, wallets, wedding rings, and

At the landfill, debris was placed on conveyor belts for workers to search through.

ID badges. Since then, most artifacts have been given to museums or returned to the families of victims.

At the landfill, workers also separated human remains from the debris. Nearly 300 bodies were found intact. More than 20,000 body parts, including bone and tissue fragments, were also recovered. Specialists then tested the remains. They hoped to identify the many people who were still missing.

The Cleanup Phase Ends

Officials estimated the Ground Zero cleanup would take a year, but it was complete in eight months. In addition to finishing ahead of schedule, no member of the crew was seriously injured. This was a positive note in an otherwise difficult, heart-wrenching process. With the wreckage cleared, a ceremony was planned to honor the victims and everyone involved in the rescue and cleanup efforts.

A Solemn Ceremony

On May 30, 2002, the ceremony at Ground Zero marked the official end of cleanup. Thousands attended. Many more watched the event on television. At 10:28 a.m., a fire bell rang, marking the time the North Tower had fallen eight months ago.

A group of police officers and firefighters carried an American flag on a stretcher to an ambulance. This symbolized the victims at Ground Zero who were not found. Then the last steel beam to be cut down from the South Tower was carried away on a semitruck. It was the final piece of debris removed from Ground Zero.

After the Last Column was cut down, many workers added their names and other messages to it.

9/11 BY THE NUMBERS

The Last Column is three and a half stories high. It weighs 58 tons (53 t).

The beam had special significance to many at the ceremony. During cleanup, firefighter George Luis Torres and construction manager Brian Lyons had marked the column with "SQ41," for Torres's Squad 41. Torres believed the remains of several Squad 41 members were buried in rubble near the column.

After it was marked with SQ41, the column became a memorial. Other firefighters wrote their squad numbers on it. Within months, it was covered in messages and photos of victims. Today, the column is known as the Last Column.

Some people working at Ground Zero wore masks, but others did not.

Chapter 4

HEALTH AND ENVIRONMENTAL IMPACTS

Although Ground Zero cleanup had finished, the WTC attacks had lasting health and environmental effects on those living in New York City. Many rescue and cleanup workers were treated for coughs, sore throats, and vision problems after working at Ground Zero. Some, such as volunteers and undocumented workers, had not had access to protective masks. Others had chosen to stop wearing masks after hearing from a government official what turned out to be an untrue message about air safety.

Air Quality

Days after the attack, Environmental Protection Agency (EPA) head Christine Todd Whitman told the public that the air in New York City was safe to breathe. Many Ground Zero workers took this to mean that it was safe to work at Ground

Zero without a protective mask. However, it was not. The dust that hung in the air was filled with dangerous substances such as asbestos and lead. These can cause respiratory diseases, digestive diseases, and cancer.

In the months and years after the attacks, people who had worked at Ground Zero began getting these diseases. So, some accused the EPA of being wrong about the air quality. Others said the EPA had misled the public to restore calm. An investigation in 2003 found that the EPA should have issued stronger warnings about the air quality. Later, Whitman apologized, saying the EPA had done its best with the information it had at the time.

Following the attacks, the EPA had established programs to test New York City's air and water for harmful dust. It had also assisted in cleaning or tearing down buildings near Ground Zero that had been contaminated. In addition, the EPA had paid for residents near Ground Zero to have their homes tested for contaminants and professionally cleaned.

Christine Todd Whitman

The EPA set up devices around Ground Zero that took samples of the air for testing.

Emotional Toll

In addition to physical health concerns, WTC survivors, Ground Zero workers, and others directly affected by the attack faced mental health issues. These included depression, anxiety, and post-traumatic stress disorder (PTSD). The highest rates of PTSD in survivors and workers occurred directly after the attacks. Those at highest risk included people who had been caught in the dust cloud after the towers collapsed. It also included those who arrived earliest at Ground Zero and stayed for long periods of time during cleanup.

Bloomberg (*left*), Giuliani (*center*), and Pataki (*right*) at the first 9/11 anniversary ceremony

Chapter 5

REMEMBERING AND REBUILDING

On September 11, 2002, the United States and the world commemorated the first anniversary of the 9/11 terrorist attacks. People held candlelight vigils throughout New York City. Thousands attended a ceremony at Ground Zero that morning. At the time, the area was fenced off in preparation for rebuilding to start.

At the ceremony, family and friends of victims held pictures of their loved ones. They placed these pictures, along with flags and flowers, in a large memorial circle at the site. Governor Pataki and newly elected New York City mayor Michael Bloomberg gave short readings. Then, former mayor Giuliani began reading aloud the names of those who died in the Twin Towers. It would take 197 readers more than two hours to finish the list.

Slow Recovery

Even a year after the attacks, businesses near Ground Zero found it difficult to move back into the area. Many had been damaged in the attacks and had to be repaired before reopening. And, some office buildings and restaurants near the site were still contaminated with debris or dust. Though some received government aid, it was often not enough to make up for lost business. It would take years for Ground Zero and the surrounding area to fully recover. However, plans to rebuild were in motion.

Daniel Libeskind

Planning a New WTC

In November 2001, Pataki and Giuliani had created the Lower Manhattan Development Corporation (LMDC). Part of the group's mission was to help plan the reconstruction of Ground Zero. This would include rebuilding many of the WTC buildings.

In February 2003, the LMDC selected Polish American architect Daniel Libeskind's design for the new WTC complex. The focal point of Libeskind's design was one large skyscraper. This building would stand 1,776 feet (541 m) high, representing the year the American colonies declared independence from Great Britain. This building was called the Freedom Tower.

Construction Delays

Construction on the Freedom Tower began in July 2004. However, the building process was put on hold due to disagreements between the developers and architects over costs and designs. And in 2005, the lower part of the building was redesigned because of security concerns of the New York City Police Department (NYPD). Many in the NYPD worried that the tower would be a prime target for another terrorist attack. One problem was that the building would be too close to the street, where large, uninspected trucks would pass by daily.

What would end up being seven years of construction on the Freedom Tower finally began in April 2006. Workers dug 200 feet (61 m) into the ground to lay supports for the building. Digging down brought grim reminders of the past. At the beginning of construction, human remains and items such as shoes and wallets were found almost every day.

One World Trade Center

In 2009, the name of the Freedom Tower was changed to One World Trade Center. Over the course of the project, 10,000 construction workers would help build the center's 104 floors. Many of these

At the time of its completion, One World Trade Center was the tallest building in the Western Hemisphere and the third tallest building in the world.

workers had family members who had built the original Twin Towers. By 2011, construction workers were completing almost one floor of the building a week.

In 2013, workers raised a 408-foot (124 m) spire on top of the tower. This made the total height of the building 1,776 feet (541 m). Construction was complete. On November 3, 2014, One World Trade Center officially opened. The building includes a restaurant, an observation deck, and dozens of floors of office space. Media company Condé Nast was the first business to move into the new building. It occupies 24 floors.

Other buildings in the WTC complex were constructed as well. The 52-story 7 World Trade Center opened in 2006. In 2013, 4 World Trade Center was completed. And, 3 World Trade Center was finished in 2018. These buildings house business offices as well as retail stores and restaurants.

Memorial and Museum

The LMDC also built a memorial at Ground Zero. In 2003, the corporation held a contest to choose a design. It received 5,201 entries from 63 countries. The winning design, submitted by Israeli American architect Michael Arad, was picked in January 2004.

Arad's memorial was called *Reflecting Absence*. It opened on September 11, 2011, the tenth anniversary of the attack. Two large, square pools mark where the Twin Towers once stood. Waterfalls along the sides of the pools send water flowing 30 feet (9 m) into each pool. The water covers the bottoms of the pools and drains through square holes in the pools' centers. Arad's waterfall design is meant to symbolize absence. While the water continuously flows down into the pools, the pools will never be filled.

The names of the 9/11 victims, as well as victims of the 1993 WTC bombing, are inscribed around the edges of the pools. The names are grouped in meaningful ways. For example, friends and

US Marines visit the pools at the 9/11 Memorial.

coworkers appear near each other, as do members of firefighting and police units.

The 9/11 Memorial Museum stands near the reflecting pools. After several construction delays, it opened to the public on May 21, 2014. The museum contains artifacts recovered from Ground Zero. It also features photos of the victims and stories from survivors.

The Last Column stands in the 9/11 Memorial Museum's main hall.

THE WORLD TRADE CENTER: THEN AND NOW

7 WTC
height: 610 feet (190 m)
floors: 47
year completed: 1987

5 WTC
height: 118 ft (36 m)
floors: 9
year completed: 1972

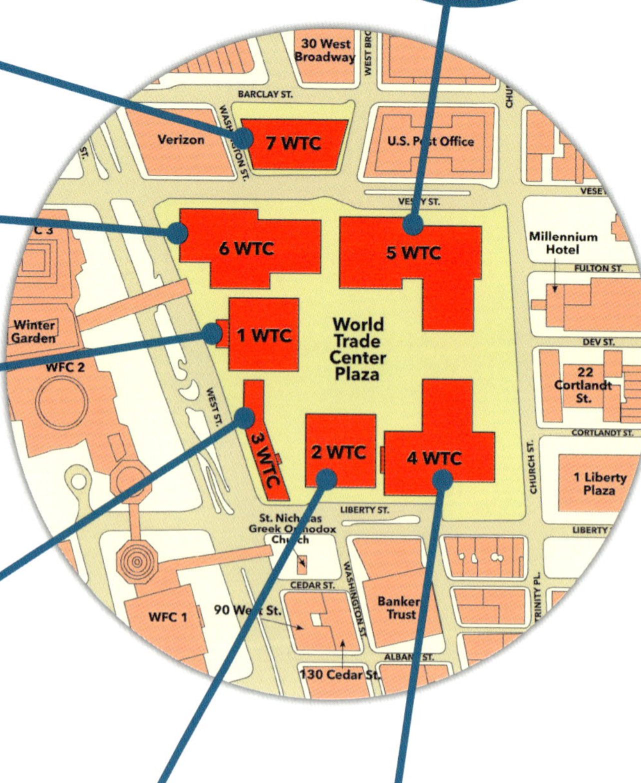

6 WTC
height: 92 feet (28 m)
floors: 8
year completed: 1973

1 WTC (NORTH TOWER)
height: 1,368 feet (417 m)
floors: 110
year completed: 1972

3 WTC
height: 242 feet (74 m)
floors: 22
year completed: 1981

2 WTC (SOUTH TOWER)
height: 1,362 feet (415 m)
floors: 110
year completed: 1973

4 WTC
height: 118 feet (36 m)
floors: 9
year completed: 1975

The 9/11 terrorist attacks destroyed all seven buildings of the WTC complex. Since then, several of them have been rebuilt. They are in slightly different locations at the WTC site, allowing the 9/11 Memorial & Museum to be where the Twin Towers once stood.

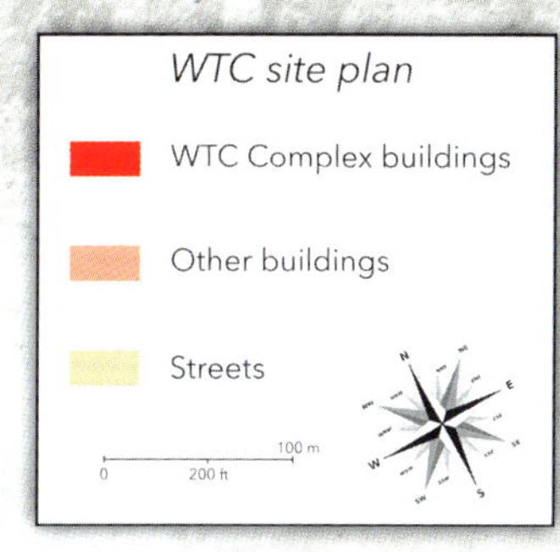

1 WTC
height: 1,776 feet (541 m)
floors: 99 (5 underground)
year completed: 2014

7 WTC
height: 743 feet (226 m)
floors: 52
year completed: 2006

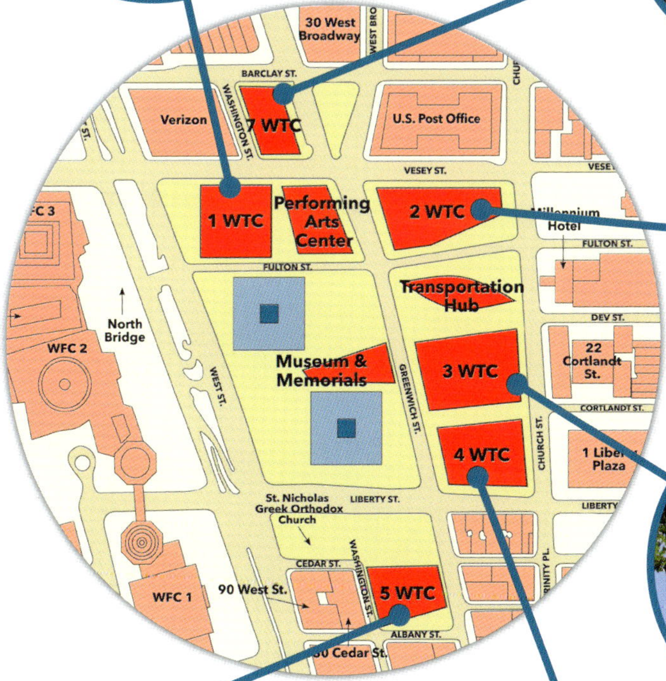

6 WTC
no new building planned

2 WTC
height: 1,323 feet (403 m)
floors: 82
year completed: 2024 (estimated)

3 WTC
height: 1,079 feet (329 m)
floors: 80
year completed: 2018

5 WTC
height: 743 feet (226 m)
floors: 42
year completed: no estimated date

4 WTC
height: 978 feet (298 m)
floors: 74
year completed: 2013

The 9/11 Memorial & Museum

Chapter 6

GROUND ZERO TODAY

The WTC attacks killed 2,753 people. In recent years, the number of victims has grown. Thousands who breathed in the dangerous dust and toxic fumes from Ground Zero have died from resulting illnesses. Tens of thousands more are sick from side effects related to exposure to the air at Ground Zero. This includes not only survivors and first responders, but also those who lived, worked, or went to school in the area.

Help for Victims

In 2001, Congress established the September 11th Victim Compensation Fund (VCF). The fund gave money to those who had been hurt or lost family members in the attacks. The VCF expired in 2004. But in 2011, it was reactivated to cover those with 9/11-related illnesses.

Reactivating the fund was part of a larger act called the James Zadroga 9/11 Health and Compensation Act of 2010. Zadroga was a police officer who died of a respiratory disease five years after working at Ground Zero. The

PIVOTAL PERSON: JAMES ZADROGA

As a first responder in New York City, James Zadroga spent more than 450 hours assisting in rescue and recovery work at Ground Zero in the weeks following the 9/11 terrorist attacks. Several weeks after his service there ended, Zadroga was treated for coughing and shortness of breath. Several months after that, he needed an oxygen tank to breathe. Zadroga died on January 5, 2006. He was the first police officer whose death was directly linked to working at Ground Zero.

act named after him also created the World Trade Center Health Program, which helps and treat patients with 9/11-related illnesses. About half of the more than 100,000 patients in the program have respiratory or digestive diseases and 18,000 have cancer. Hundreds of people have died from these diseases. In Spring 2019, a Memorial Glade was added to the 9/11 Memorial at Ground Zero in their honor.

President Barack Obama signed the Zadroga Act in Hawaii on January 2, 2011.

Identifying Remains

As of 2020, efforts were still underway to identify all of the people who died at Ground Zero. About 40 percent of victims have not been identified through remains found at the site. Many of the remains are bone fragments, from which it is difficult to extract DNA. The identification process continues as more advanced methods are developed. In the meantime, many families who lost loved ones at Ground Zero are still waiting for official evidence to confirm the deaths.

Construction Continues

Today, New York City's skyline is filled with the new, shimmering glass buildings of the WTC. Although the wreckage has long been cleared, many still refer to the site as Ground Zero. Every day, Ground Zero continues to change. In January 2020, New York governor Andrew Cuomo announced intentions to rebuild a church that was destroyed in the attacks by September 11, 2021. And the new 2 WTC building is scheduled for completion in 2022.

Special Events

The 9/11 Memorial & Museum hosts events at Ground Zero. One is a 5K Run/Walk and Community Day. This event was first held in 2013. Every April, it commemorates the 9/11 victims and celebrates New York City's strength. It also raises money through registration fees, corporate sponsorships, and donations from participants to help keep the museum running. The 5K course winds along the

Thousands of runners participate in the 5K Run/Walk each year.

"Hero Highway" near the WTC. This was the route taken by workers to get to Ground Zero during cleanup efforts. Crowds would gather along the street to cheer for and encourage the workers.

After the 5K, people are invited to remain at the memorial to paint wooden stars as part of the Stars of HOPE healing arts program. This program was started in 2007 by the charitable organization New York Says Thank You Foundation. Stars of HOPE sends stars painted with inspiring, hopeful messages to people around the world affected by disasters. In 2019, the stars painted at Community Day were given to first responders, healthcare providers, victims' families, and others during the Memorial Glade's dedication. The 5K Run/Walk and Community Day was canceled in 2020 due to the COVID-19 pandemic. But plans were underway to hold it again in 2021.

Memories Live On

Memorial ceremonies are held yearly at Ground Zero. At these ceremonies, the names of the victims from the 9/11 terrorist attacks and the 1993 WTC bombing are read aloud. The WTC attacks are also commemorated by the Tribute in Light. During this annual public art display, two beams of bright blue light near the WTC shine four miles (6 km) into the sky, representing the Twin Towers.

The 9/11 terrorist attacks are fresh in the minds of many who witnessed them. Younger generations, however, may view the attacks as distant history. The memorial and museum at Ground Zero ensure that all visitors, no matter their ages, will never forget the day's events and aftermath. Although New York City continues to rebuild, the memories of the 9/11 terrorist attacks and those who died that day will forever live on at Ground Zero.

The Tribute in Light

TIMELINE

SEPTEMBER 11, 2001

Two of four airplanes hijacked by terrorists are purposefully flown into the Twin Towers in New York City. Both towers collapse, killing thousands of people.

SEPTEMBER 14, 2001

President Bush gives an unplanned speech at Ground Zero, energizing rescue workers.

NOVEMBER 2001

Governor Pataki and Mayor Giuliani create the Lower Manhattan Development Corporation (LMDC) to plan the reconstruction of Ground Zero.

2002
Cleanup at Ground Zero officially ends on May 30. The first annual ceremony to honor the 9/11 victims is held on September 11.

2003
In February, The LMDC selects a design for the new WTC complex.

2004
The LMDC selects a design for the 9/11 memorial at Ground Zero.

2006
Construction on the Freedom Tower, later named One World Trade Center, begins.

2010
Congress passes the James Zadroga 9/11 Health and Compensation Act of 2010.

2011
The memorial *Reflecting Absence* opens at Ground Zero on the tenth anniversary of the 9/11 terrorist attacks.

2013
Construction of One World Trade Center is completed.

2014
On May 21, the 9/11 Memorial Museum opens at Ground Zero. One World Trade Center opens on November 3.

2020
Efforts to identify victims of the 9/11 terrorist attacks through DNA testing continue.

GLOSSARY

aftermath—the time immediately following a bad and usually destructive event.

architect—a person who plans and designs buildings.

artifact—an object remaining from a particular location or time period.

asbestos—minerals that builders once used to fireproof buildings. Today, scientists know that breathing in asbestos fibers can cause diseases such as cancer.

commemorate—to honor and remember an important person or event.

digestive—of or relating to the breakdown of food into simpler substances the body can absorb.

dispatcher—a person whose job is to send someone or something to a particular place for a particular purpose.

DNA—deoxyribonucleic acid. A material in the body that is different in every person except identical twins. Scientists can extract DNA from blood or hair found at a crime scene. This information can help identify people.

extract—to withdraw by a physical or chemical process.

hangar—a building where aircraft are kept and repaired.

hijack—to take over by threatening violence.

Islam—the religion of Muslims as described in the Koran. Islam is based on the teachings of the god Allah through the prophet Muhammad.

landfill—a system used for garbage disposal. Trash is layered with earth to build up an area of land.

memorial—something that serves to remind people of a person or an event.

Muslim—a person who follows Islam.

pandemic—an occurrence in which a disease spreads very quickly and affects many people over a large area.

paramedic—someone trained to care for a patient before or during the trip to a hospital.

Pentagon—the five-sided building near Washington, DC, where the main offices of the US Department of Defense are located.

post-traumatic stress disorder (PTSD)—a mental condition that can be caused by a very shocking or difficult experience. Symptoms of PTSD include depression and anxiety.

respiratory—having to do with the system of organs involved with breathing.

vigil—a gathering during which people stay in place and quietly wait or pray.

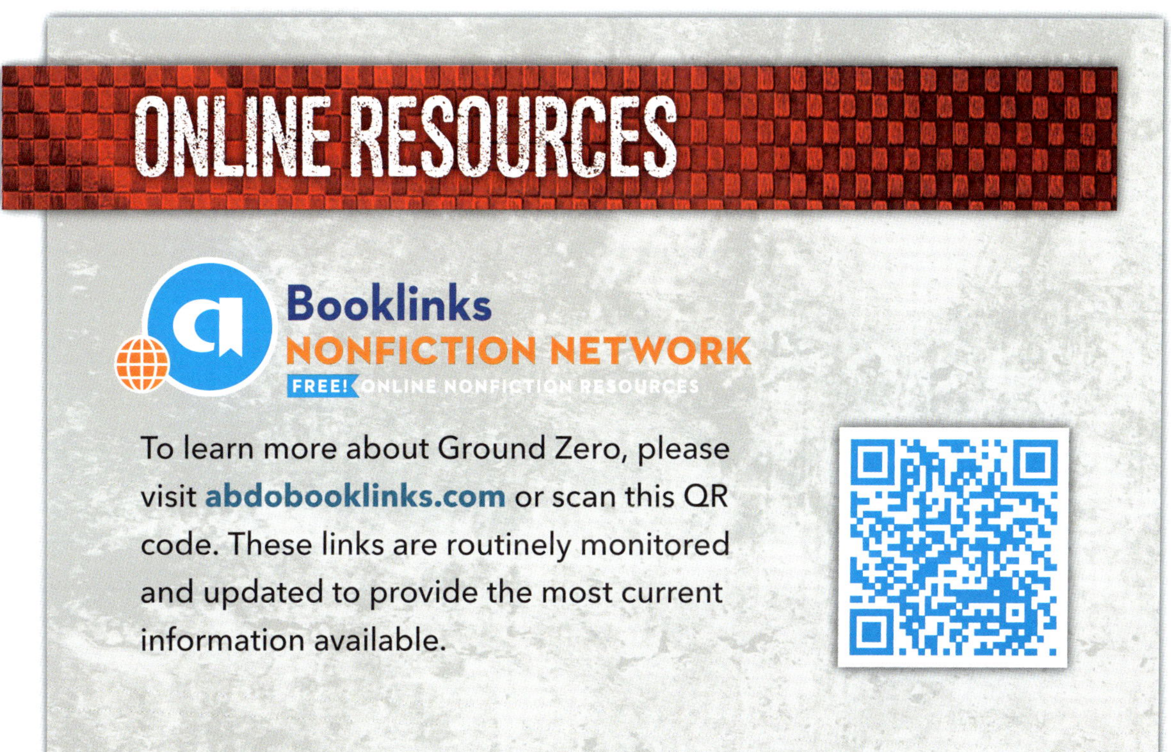

INDEX